**LITTLE TIGER**

LONDON

CATERPILLAR BOOKS
An imprint of the Little Tiger Group
www.littletiger.co.uk
1 Coda Studios, 189 Munster Road, London SW6 6AW
First published in Great Britain 2021
Text by Isabel Otter • Text copyright © Caterpillar Books Ltd. 2021
Illustrations copyright © Fernando Martín 2021
A CIP catalogue record for this book is available from the British Library
All rights reserved • Printed in China
ISBN: 978-1-83891-046-4
CPB/1400/1640/1120
2 4 6 8 10 9 7 5 3 1

The Forest Stewardship Council® (FSC®) is an international, non-governmental organisation dedicated to promoting responsible management of the world's forests. FSC operates a system of forest certification and product labelling that allows consumers to identify wood and wood-based products from well-managed forests and other controlled sources.

For more information about the FSC, please visit their website at www.fsc.org

FSC® C104723
MIX
Paper from responsible sources

# I am a FiSH

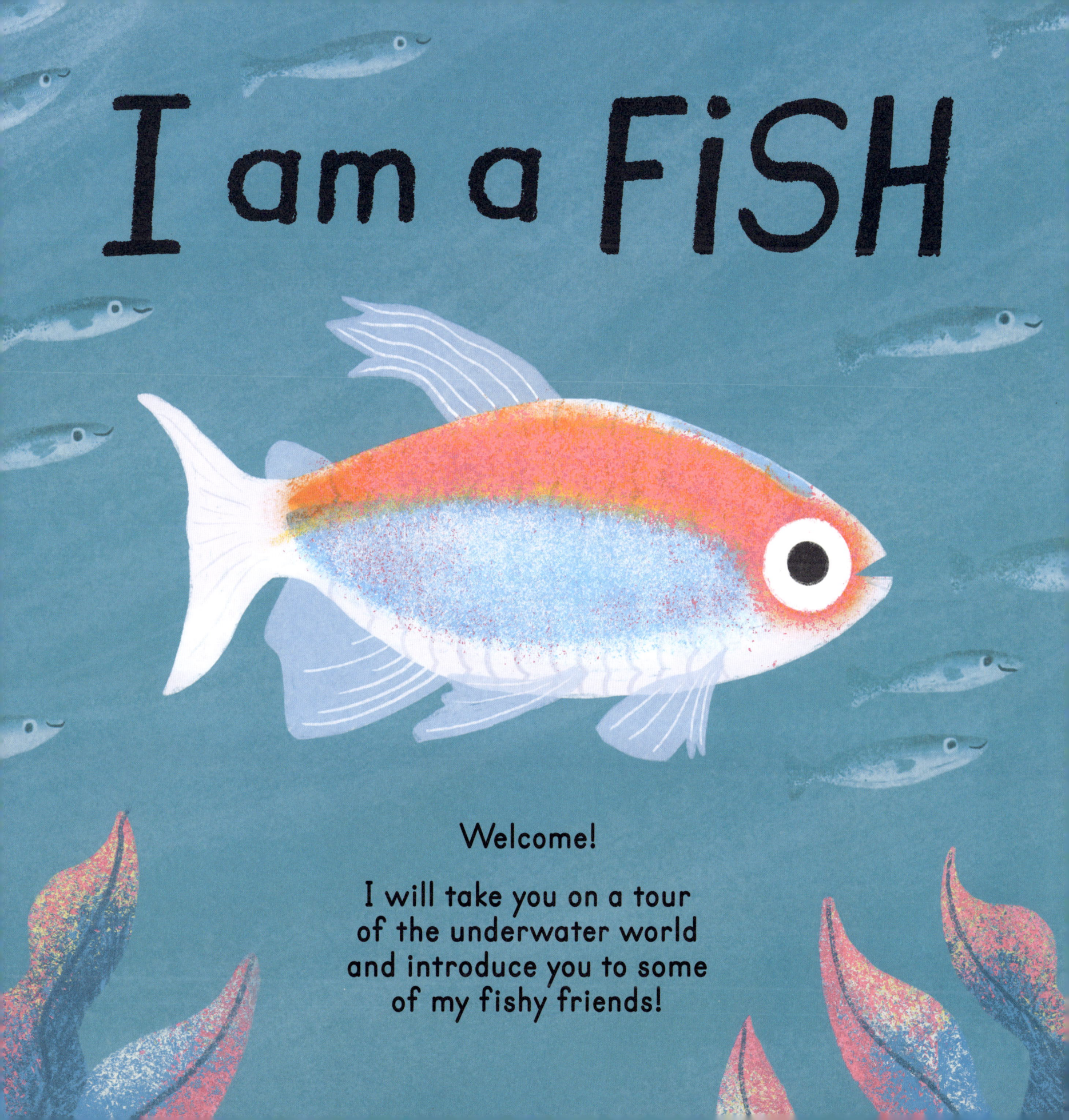

Welcome!

I will take you on a tour of the underwater world and introduce you to some of my fishy friends!

I don't have eyelids, so I never need to blink. My eyes stay open all the time.

I can breathe **underwater!** I suck water in and it passes through my gills, which are like lungs.

gills

fin

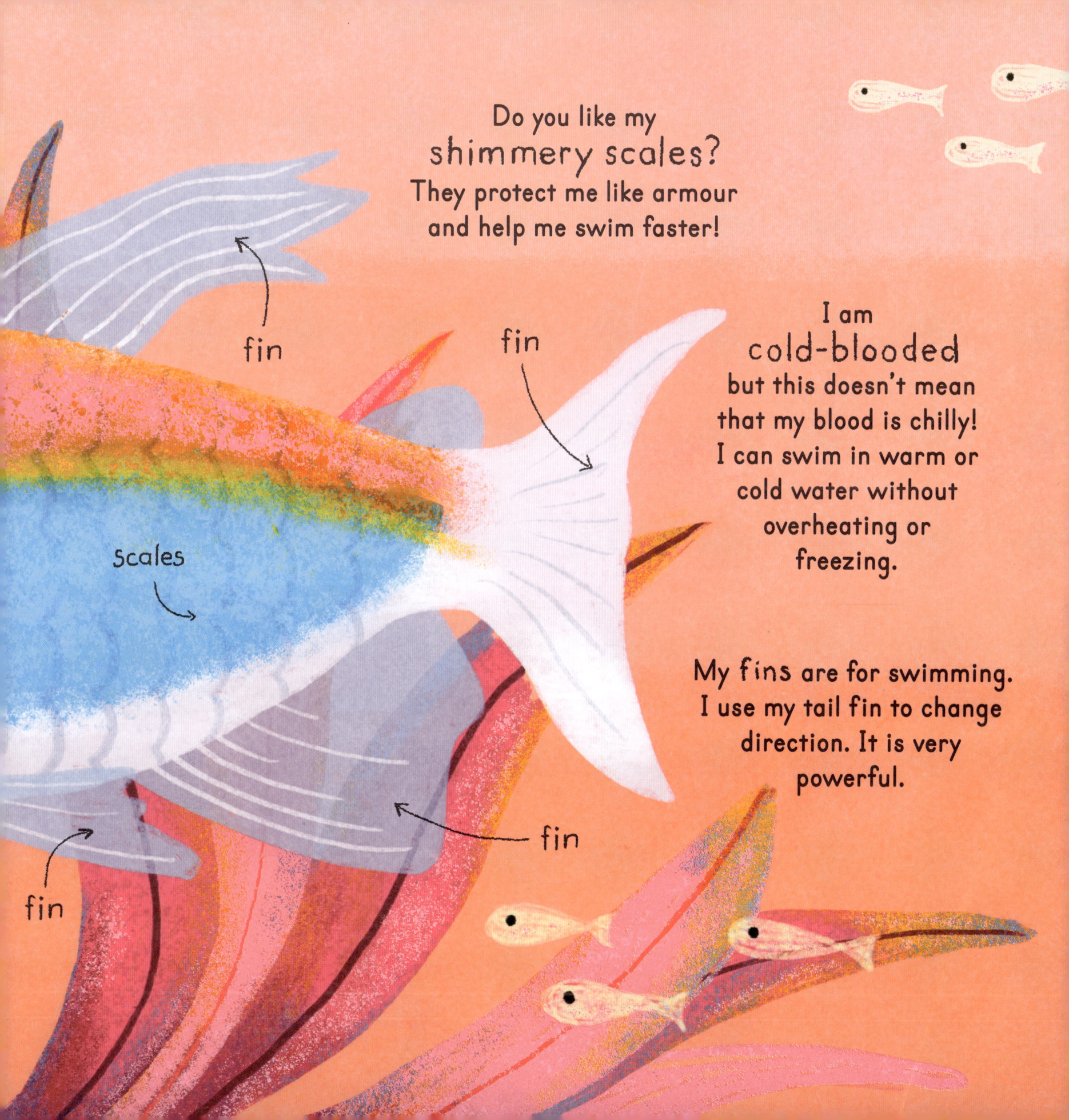

Do you like my **shimmery scales?** They protect me like armour and help me swim faster!

I am **cold-blooded** but this doesn't mean that my blood is chilly! I can swim in warm or cold water without overheating or freezing.

My fins are for swimming. I use my tail fin to change direction. It is very powerful.

fin

fin

scales

fin

fin

# Where do fish live?

Most fish spend their lives in the sea, where the water is salty.

These clownfish live with an animal called an anemone. Its stinging tentacles keep them safe from predators.

In return, the clownfish ward off butterflyfish, who would otherwise eat the anemone.

Kelp forests are made from giant stems of seaweed. Rockfish like to live there, bobbing in the floating leaves. They can live to be 200 years old!

Some fish live...

deep,

deep

down

at the bottom of the sea.

It is extremely **cold** and **dark** down there.

Only the hardiest can survive, such as this bright blue wolf fish!

Other fish live in freshwater lakes, streams or rivers.

Most catfish like fast-moving rivers. They can grow to be longer than a person!

Do you know how they got their name? The clue is in the whiskers!

# Baby fish hatch out of eggs

Most fish lay thousands of eggs at a time.

The eggs are laid in clusters. They are like little balls of jelly.

When the baby fish are ready, they burst out of their eggs and look like this.

Once young fish are able to feed themselves they are known as 'fry'.

Most fish swim in groups

Fish are sociable and many like to swim in crowds called **shoals**.

If all the fish in a shoal are swimming in the same direction it's called a **school**.

Fish are safer from predators when they swim together.

But some fish, such as this barracuda, prefer to swim alone.

# Do fish sleep?

Fish take periods of rest but do not sleep deeply like humans.

Their eyes remain open and they stay alert. This helps them to avoid getting eaten!

Some fish rest while floating, or dig themselves a little hole in the sand.

Others lodge themselves between rocks or corals...

Zzzzz

...so they don't float away!

# What do fish eat?

Some fish are **herbivores**.

This means that they eat plants and like to munch on delicious algae and seaweed.

Other fish are **carnivores.**

They are meat-eaters who like to prey on small creatures such as shrimp, or if you're a shark — other fish!

# Which is the smallest fish?

We cannot say for certain because so few of the smallest species have been found, but the **stout infantfish** is one of the tiniest. It is smaller than the nail of your little finger.

Blink and you'll miss it!

It lives in warm, tropical waters in Australia's Great Barrier Reef and the Coral Sea.

The stout infantfish is unusual because it does not have any teeth or scales.

Its lifespan is just two months.

# Meet the biggest fish

Whale sharks are larger than any other fish. They can grow to be the length of a bus!

Every whale shark has a pattern
of spots that is unique —
like a human fingerprint.

They are carnivores, but whale sharks don't chase their prey.
Instead, they open their mouths wide and suck up everything
in their path, sieving out the things they don't want to eat!

# Fish come in all shapes and sizes!

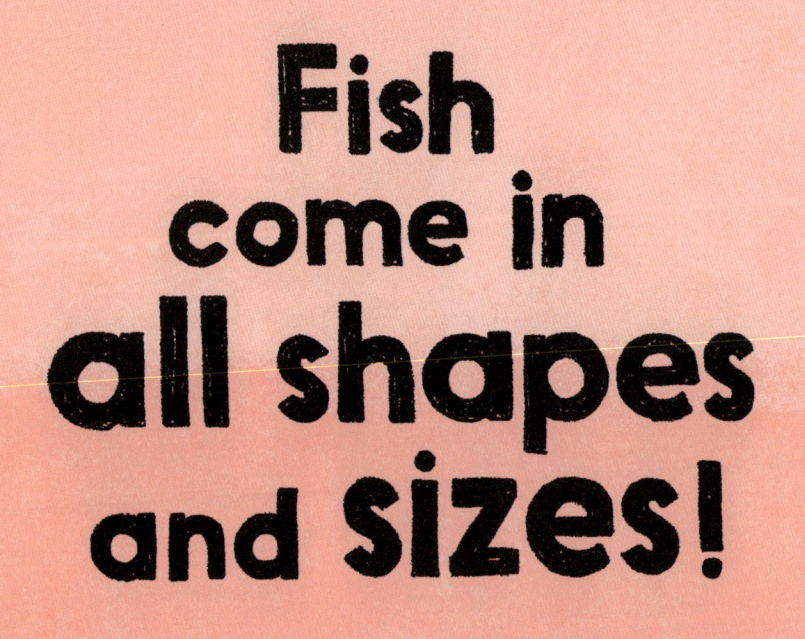

Rays don't have bones. They swim using their 'wings'. Some rays are just the size of a baby's hand, while others are longer than a giraffe is tall!

Most sharks are fierce hunters with rows of sharp, jagged teeth for attacking prey.

Eels have long, thin bodies that they wriggle to propel themselves through the water.

# We are fish too!

**Seahorses** use their tails to anchor themselves to corals, sea grasses or even each other!

Some couples dance together every day to strengthen their bond.

Male seahorses give birth. They carry the babies in a pouch until they are ready for life on their own.

Some seahorses can change colour to blend in with their surroundings when they sense danger.

# Look at our rainbow of colours!

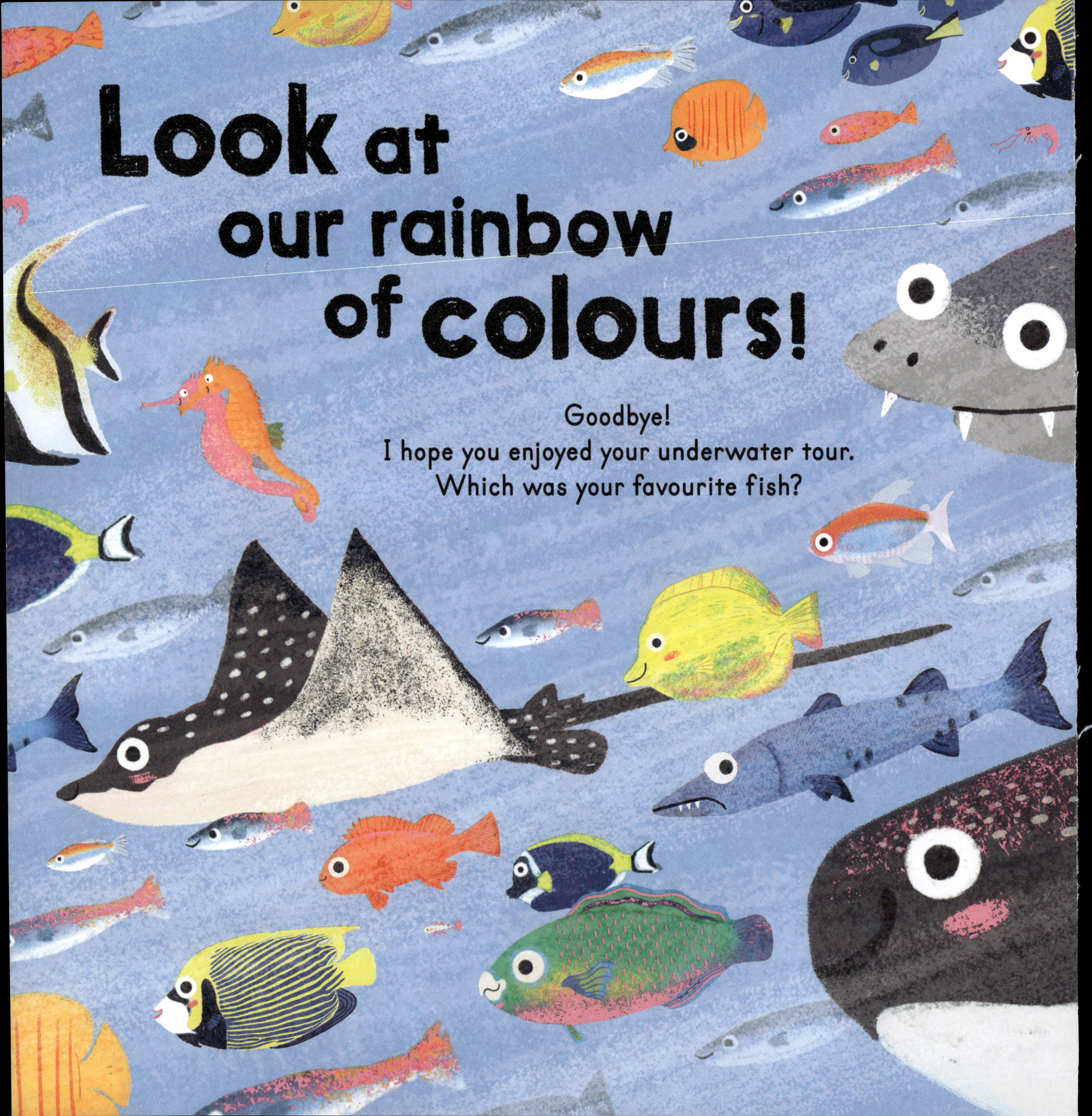

Goodbye!
I hope you enjoyed your underwater tour.
Which was your favourite fish?